Marshall

by Iain Gray

D1270093

LangSyne
PUBLISHING
WRITING *to* REMEMBER

LangSyne

PUBLISHING

WRITING *to* REMEMBER

Vineyard Business Centre,
Pathhead, Midlothian EH37 5XP
Tel: 01875 321 203 Fax: 01875 321 233
E-mail: info@lang-syne.co.uk
www.langsyneshop.co.uk

Design by Dorothy Meikle
Printed by Ricoh Print Scotland
© Lang Syne Publishers Ltd 2010

ISBN 978-1-85217-368-5

Marshall

MOTTO:
By virtue safe.

CREST:
A dove and olive branch
(and)
The head of a griffin.

NAME variations include:
Marescal
Marescall
Marshal
Marshale
Marischal
Merchel
Mershell

Echoes of a far distant past
can still be found in most names

Chapter one:

Origins of Scottish surnames

by George Forbes

It all began with the Normans.

For it was they who introduced surnames into common usage more than a thousand years ago, initially based on the title of their estates, local villages and chateaux in France to distinguish and identify these landholdings, usually acquired at the point of a bloodstained sword.

Such grand descriptions also helped enhance the prestige of these arrogant warlords and generally glorify their lofty positions high above the humble serfs slaving away below in the pecking order who only had single names, often with Biblical connotations as in Pierre and Jacques.

The only descriptive distinctions among this peasantry concerned their occupations, like Pierre the swineherd or Jacques the ferryman.

The Normans themselves were originally Vikings (or Northmen) who raided, colonised and eventually settled down around the French coastline.

They had sailed up the Seine in their longboats in 900 AD under their ferocious leader Rollo and ruled the roost in north east France before sailing over to conquer England, bringing their relatively new tradition of having surnames with them.

It took another hundred years for the Normans to percolate northwards and surnames did not begin to appear in Scotland until the thirteenth century.

These adventurous knights brought an aura of chivalry with them and it was said no damsel of any distinction would marry a man unless he had at least two names.

The family names included that of Scotland's great hero Robert De Brus and his compatriots were warriors from families like the De Morevils, De Umphravils, De Berkelais, De Quincis, De Viponts and De Vaux.

As the knights settled the boundaries of their vast estates, they took territorial names, as in Hamilton, Moray, Crawford, Cunningham, Dunbar, Ross, Wemyss, Dundas, Galloway, Renfrew, Greenhill, Hazelwood, Sandylands and Church-hill.

Other names, though not with any obvious geographical or topographical features, nevertheless derived from ancient parishes like Douglas, Forbes, Dalyell and Guthrie.

Other surnames were coined in connection with occupations, castles or legendary deeds. Stuart originated in the word steward, a prestigious post which was an integral part of any large medieval household. The same applied to Cooks, Chamberlains, Constables and Porters.

Borders towns and forts – needed in areas like the Debateable Lands which were constantly fought over by feuding local families – had their own distinctive names; and it was often from them that the resident groups took their communal titles, as in the Grahams of Annandale, the Elliots and Armstrongs of the East Marches, the Scotts and Kerrs of Teviotdale and Eskdale.

Even physical attributes crept into surnames, as in Small, Little and More (the latter being 'beg' in Gaelic), Long or Lang, Stark, Stout, Strong or Strang and even Jolly.

Mieklejohns would have had the strength of several men, while Littlejohn was named after the legendary sidekick of Robin Hood.

Colours got into the act with Black, White, Grey, Brown and Green (Red developed into Reid,

Ruddy or Ruddiman). Blue was rare and nobody ever wanted to be associated with yellow.

Pompous worthies took the name Wiseman, Goodman and Goodall.

Words intimating the sons of leading figures were soon affiliated into the language as in Johnson, Adamson, Richardson and Thomson, while the Norman equivalent of Fitz (from the French-Latin 'filius' meaning 'son') cropped up in Fitzmaurice and Fitzgerald.

The prefix 'Mac' was 'son of' in Gaelic and clans often originated with occupations – as in MacNab being sons of the Abbot, MacPherson and MacVicar being sons of the minister and MacIntosh being sons of the chief.

The church's influence could be found in the names Kirk, Clerk, Clarke, Bishop, Friar and Monk. Proctor came from a church official, Singer and Sangster from choristers, Gilchrist and Gillies from Christ's servant, Mitchell, Gilmory and Gilmour from servants of St Michael and Mary, Malcolm from a servant of Columba and Gillespie from a bishop's servant.

The rudimentary medical profession was represented by Barber (a trade which also once included dentistry and surgery) as well as Leech or Leitch.

Businessmen produced Merchants, Mercers, Monypennies, Chapmans, Sellers and Scales, while down at the old village watermill the names that cropped up included Miller, Walker and Fuller.

Other self explanatory trades included Coopers, Brands, Barkers, Tanners, Skinners, Brewsters and Brewers, Tailors, Saddlers, Wrights, Cartwrights, Smiths, Harpers, Joiners, Sawyers, Masons and Plumbers.

Even the scenery was utilised as in Craig, Moor, Hill, Glen, Wood and Forrest.

Rank, whether high or low, took its place with Laird, Barron, Knight, Tennant, Farmer, Husband, Granger, Grieve, Shepherd, Shearer and Fletcher.

The hunt and the chase supplied Hunter, Falconer, Fowler, Fox, Forrester, Archer and Spearman.

The renowned medieval historian Froissart, who eulogised about the romantic deeds of chivalry (and who condemned Scotland as being a poverty stricken wasteland), once sniffily dismissed the peasantry of his native France as the jacquerie (or the jacques-without-names) but it was these same humble folk who ended up overthrowing the arrogant aristocracy.

In the olden days, only the blueblooded knights of antiquity were entitled to full, proper names, both Christian and surnames, but with the passing of time and a more egalitarian, less feudal atmosphere, more respectful and worthy titles spread throughout the populace as a whole.

Echoes of a far distant past can still be found in most names and they can be borne with pride in commemoration of past generations who fought and toiled in some capacity or other to make our nation what it now is, for good or ill.

Chapter two:

For God and Covenant

Ranked 51st in the list of Scotland's most common surnames, Marshall is a name found from the Borders to the Highlands and Islands.

Also found throughout the world in the form of a number of variations, it derives from the French word 'maréchal', originally indicating 'horse servant' or 'tender of horses'.

In common with many surnames, as noted in *Chapter one*, it was first introduced to British shores in the wake of the Norman Conquest of the island in 1066, with bearers of the name serving the important role of tending the horses of the nobility.

Through time, the form of 'Marischal' developed in Scotland as a title for the person charged with the custody of the nation's Royal Regalia of sceptre, crown and sword, also known as the Honours of Scotland, and for the protection of the monarch in Parliament. It is from this that a very confusing link between the Marshalls and the more-powerful Clan Keith developed.

The Keiths take their name from the lands of

Keith, in East Lothian, where they appear to have first settled in the twelfth century during the reign of Scotland's David I, later acquiring more lands throughout the nation, particularly in Buchan in the far north east.

It was in East Lothian that a family of Marshalls also appear to have first settled, arriving from the English county of Wiltshire.

A close kinship developed between the Marshalls and the Keiths, in all probability through marriage, and it is perhaps no more than strange coincidence that the Keith chieftains later assumed the hereditary title of 'Great Marischal' or 'Earl Marischal' of Scotland.

The honoured title was conferred on the Keiths as hereditary by the warrior king Robert the Bruce following his victory at the battle of Bannockburn in 1314 – a battle at which the Great Marischal Sir Robert Keith commanded a force of 500 cavalry and in which his kinsfolk such as the Marshals would also have fought.

A battle that involved the defeat of a 20,000-strong English army under Edward II by a Scots army less than half this strength, it was through a misguided sense of chivalry that it occurred in the first place.

By midsummer of 1313 the mighty fortress of Stirling Castle was occupied by an English garrison under the command of Sir Philip Mowbray.

Bruce's hot-headed brother, Edward, agreed to a pledge by Mowbray that if the castle was not relieved by battle by midsummer of the following year, then he would surrender.

This made battle inevitable, and by June 23 of 1314 the two armies faced one another at Bannockburn, in sight of the castle.

It was on this day that Bruce slew the English knight Sir Henry de Bohun in single combat, but the battle proper was not fought until the following day, shortly after the rise of the midsummer sun.

The English cavalry launched a desperate but futile charge on the densely packed ranks of Scottish spearmen known as schiltrons, and by the time the sun had sank slowly in the west the English army had been totally routed, with Edward himself only narrowly managing to make his escape from the carnage of the battlefield.

Whatever the origins and circumstances of the bond between the Marshalls and the Keiths, it should be stressed that 'Marischal' was a *title* conferred on the Keiths, not a name.

So close is the bond, however, that the Marshalls, along with clans that include the Austens, Dicksons, Falconers and Harveys, are considered a sept, or branch, of the Keiths – whose own proud motto is 'Truth conquers' and whose crest is a roebuck's head emerging out of a crown coronet.

The Marshalls first step onto the pages of Scotland's voluminous historical record nearly 180 years before the battle of Bannockburn, with a Maledoni Marescal recorded as having witnessed a charter in Glasgow in 1136.

Later in the same century, Gillecolm Marescald is on record as having witnessed a charter in the ecclesiastical town of St Andrews.

Being witness to important charters indicates a high level of social standing, and another example of the status of at least some of the bearers of the Marshall name – in all its early variations – comes from the infamous Ragman Roll of 1296.

It was in July of that year that the Scots rose in revolt against the imperialist designs of the English king Edward I, but, living up to his reputation of 'Hammer of the Scots', he brought the entire nation under his subjugation little less than a month later.

To reinforce his domination, 1,500 earls, bishops and burgesses were required to sign a humiliating treaty of fealty, known as the Ragman Roll, because of the profusion of ribbons that dangled from the seals of the reluctant signatories – a number of Marshalls among them.

The very landscape of Scotland bears silent witness to the terrible convulsions that ripped the nation apart nearly 400 years later as a bitter and bloody war raged between Crown and Covenant – a civil war in which many Marshalls are recorded as having carried the banner of '*For God and Covenant*'.

Nestled in the bosom of some of the wildest and most inaccessible spots of Galloway, Dumfriesshire, Lanarkshire and Ayrshire are memorials to those who chose the side of the Covenant in opposition to royal claims of supremacy in matters of religion.

A National Covenant, pledging defence of the Presbyterian religion, had been signed in the Greyfriars Kirkyard, in Edinburgh, in February of 1638.

Copies were circulated throughout the length and breadth of Scotland, and the hundreds of ordinary men and women who subscribed to it became known as Covenanters.

Following the restoration to the throne of

Charles II in 1660, the death knell for the Covenanting movement was sounded when a Recissory Act was passed, declaring the Covenant illegal.

Episcopal rule was foisted on the Scottish Church, and all ministers who refused to adhere to this new order were deprived of their parishes.

Along with their congregations, many ministers literally took to the hills, preaching at open-air meetings known as conventicles, and one of the most famous of these conventicle sites was at the farm of Marshall of Starryshaw, near Shotts, in Lanarkshire.

Lookouts were posted at the conventicles to keep a wary eye out for the approach of Government troops, and justice was executed on the spot for those unfortunate enough to fall into their hands.

Many of the memorials scattered across the hills and valleys of Lowland Scotland mark the very spots where victims were summarily shot and unceremoniously buried.

Constantly persecuted by the forces of authority, the Covenanters rose in futile rebellion in November of 1666 and, as a sign of the harsh treatment that was to be subsequently meted out to them, many of the prisoners taken were tortured and hanged.

Victory followed at the battle of Drumclog in

June of 1679, only to be followed a few short weeks later by resounding defeat at the battle of Bothwell Brig, near Hamilton, by a force commanded by the Duke of Monmouth.

Nearly 800 Covenanters were killed and 1,400 taken prisoner.

Kept for several weeks in open cages in the Greyfriars Kirkyard, those who agreed to sign a bond for future 'good behaviour' were released, but by November of 1679, 340 steadfastly recalcitrant prisoners still remained.

The authorities hit upon a rather profitable solution to the problem posed by these prisoners – to sell them as slaves to what were then the colonies of America and the steaming plantations of Barbados.

Among those Covenanters transported to America for refusing to sign the bond were Marshall of Starryshaw's two sons Thomas and John, while his third son, Robert, was later freed from imprisonment after reluctantly agreeing to sign.

There is also a record from June of 1684 concerning the transportation from the Clyde to America of the Covenanters John and Thomas Marshall, from the village of Strathaven, in Lanarkshire, and who it is reasonable to assume may have been related.

Chapter three:

Gypsies and generals

One of the most infamous Scottish bearers of the Marshall name was the Ayrshire-born Billy Marshall, reputed to have been 120 years of age when he died in 1792.

Known as 'King of the Gypsies', or 'King of the Randies', his long life was certainly eventful.

Born into gypsy stock, a famed boxer, a deserter from the navy on three separate occasions and from the army seven times, the whisky swilling Marshall was also married on no less than 17 occasions, fathering an innumerable brood of children both in and out of wedlock.

As 'King of the Gypsies' of Carrick and Galloway throughout most of the 1700s, he was also a robber and smuggler and reputed to have been responsible for the murder of at least four people, while he was also a leader of what were known as Levellers – who knocked down stone walls erected by landowners to enclose their property.

His grave can be seen to this day in St Cuthbert's churchyard in the royal burgh of

Kirkcudbright, in Dumfries and Galloway, where visitors traditionally place a coin on his gravestone for the next gypsy who passes by.

One rather more respectable bearer of the Marshall name was the fiddle player and composer William Marshall, described by Scotland's national bard Robert Burns as "the first composer of strathspeys of the age."

Known as a 'Jock-of-all trades', excelling in such diverse skills as music, clock making, falconry, fishing, athletics, astronomy and architecture, he was born in 1748 in Fochabers, Morayshire, and served for more than 40 years as butler and house steward to the Duke of Gordon at Gordon Castle.

Credited with the composition of nearly 260 fiddle tunes, including the strathspeys *The Marchioness of Huntly*, *Lady Madelina Sinclair* and *The Nameless Lassie*, and a setting for the Burns poem *Of a' the airts the wind can blaw*, he died in 1833.

Born in Edinburgh 20 years before the death of William Marshall, William Calder Marshall was the distinguished Scottish sculptor who studied at the Royal Academy School in London, where he won its prestigious silver medal, and in Rome.

Before his death in 1894 he was responsible for the decoration of a range of noted London edifices that include the Houses of Parliament, Westminster Abbey, St Paul's Cathedral and the Albert Memorial.

Those Marshalls and their descendants who established new lives for themselves on foreign shores contributed greatly, and continue to do so, to the life of the nations in which they settled.

Not least among them was John Marshall, who served as 4th Chief Justice of the United States from 1801 to 1835, making him, to date, the longest serving Chief Justice in the history of the United States Supreme Court.

Born in 1755 in Germantown, Virginia, Marshall, who died in 1835, is recognised as having helped to shape American Constitutional Law and for making the Supreme Court the vital centre of decision-making that it is today.

The town of Marshall, in Michigan, is named in his honour.

No less distinguished, but in another sphere, was his descendant General George Catlett Marshall, the great American soldier who made a significant contribution to the victory of the Allies in the Second World War.

Born in 1880 in Uniontown, Pennsylvania, and described by the British wartime leader Winston Churchill as the "organiser of victory", he served as U.S. Chief of Army Staff throughout the war and as chief military adviser to American President Franklin D. Roosevelt.

Graduating from the Virginia Military Academy in 1901 and serving with distinction on the Western Front during the First World War, his skills came particularly to the fore in the Second World War when he played a vital role in preparing both the U.S. Army and U.S. Air Force for the invasion of Hitler's 'Fortress Europe' in the summer of 1944.

The recipient of a host of honours that include two Distinguished Service Medals and a Silver Star, he also served as Secretary of State under President Harry S. Truman from 1947 to 1949 and Secretary of Defense under the same president from 1950 to 1951.

He was also the first American general to be promoted, in December of 1944, to the five star rank of General of the Army

The originator of the Marshall Plan to restore a devastated Europe after the war, he was accordingly awarded the Nobel Peace Prize in 1953.

The general, who died in 1959, is buried in Washington's Arlington National Cemetery.

Also on the battlefield, James Marshall was an English recipient of the Victoria Cross, the highest award for bravery for British and Commonwealth forces.

Born in 1887, he had been serving during the First World War with the Irish Guards, attached to the Lancashire Fusiliers, when he was killed only days before the end of the conflict in November 1918.

This was while rallying his comrades to repair a vital bridge crossing near Catillon, in France.

Chapter four:

On the world stage

Away from the battlefield, bearers of the Marshall name have gained distinction in a range of other endeavours.

Born in 1914 in Owatonna, Minnesota, **E.G. Marshall** was the American radio, film and television actor who, early in his career, legally changed his given name of Everett Eugene Grunz to Everett Gillespie Marshall.

His television roles included that of the lawyer Lawrence Preston in the popular legal drama *The Defenders*, while from 1974 to 1982 he was the host of the equally popular radio drama The *CBS Radio Mystery Theater*.

Films in which he starred include the 1957 *Twelve Angry Men*, the 1969 *The Bridge at Remagen* and, a year before his death in 1998, *Absolute Power*.

Best known for his co-direction, along with John Ford and Henry Hathaway, of the epic 1962 *How the West Was Won*, **George Marshall** was the film producer, director and screenwriter who was born in Chicago in 1891 and died in 1975.

His other notable film credits include *Destry Rides Again*, from 1939, and the 1969 *Hook, Line and Sinker*.

Born in 1943 in the Bronx area of New York, **Penny Marshall** is the American director, producer and actress whose immigrant father changed his name from the Italian 'Marsciarelli' to Marshall.

The actress, who is part Scottish through her mother, is best known for her role between 1976 and 1983 as Laverne De Falio in the top American sitcom *Laverne and Shirley* – for which she won no less than three Golden Globe nominations.

Her film directing credits include the 1988 *Big* and the 1992 *A League of their Own*, while in 2005 she produced *Cinderella Man*.

Keeping it in the family, her brother **Garry Marshall**, born in 1934, is the actor, director, producer and writer who was responsible for creating the sitcom *Happy Days*, which ran from 1974 to 1984, while his film directing credits include the 1990 *Pretty Woman* and the 2001 *The Princess Diaries*.

Born in 1974, **Tony Marshall** is the British television actor whose roles include the medical drama *Casualty* and the police drama *Life on Mars*, while Henry Tomasso is the veteran Scottish entertainer of Italian descent better known as **Larry Marshall**.

Born in 1924 and a talented product of Scottish music hall variety, he is best known as the compére of the daily Scottish Television show *The One O'Clock Gang*, which ran from 1957 until 1965.

Still on the stage, **Kris Marshall** is the English actor who was born in 1973 and is best known for his role as Nick Harper in the BBC sitcom *My Family*, while **James Marshall**, born in New York in 1967, is the American actor best known for his role as James Hurley in the early 1990s' cult television series *Twin Peaks*.

In a different film genre, **John Marshall** was the American anthropologist and documentary filmmaker who was born in 1932 in Cambridge, Massachusetts.

Marshall, who died in 2005, was particularly renowned for his film documentation of the tribes of the Kalahari Desert.

Also behind the camera lens, **Frank Marshall** is the American film producer and director whose many credits include the award-winning 2008 *The Curious Case of Benjamin Button* and who, along with his wife Kathleen Kennedy, is a founder of Kennedy Marshall Productions.

Born in 1946 in Los Angeles, he is a son of the composer **Jack Marshall**, who was born in 1921 and died in 1973 and whose compositions include the theme and incidental music for the 1960s' television series *The Munsters*.

Also in the creative world of music, **Larry Marshall** is the reggae musician born in Jamaica in 1941; in addition to a successful solo career, he has also enjoyed international success as a member of the duos Larry and Alvin and Larry and Enid.

Behind the drum kit, **John Marshall** is the American percussionist, born in 1954, who has worked with artistes that include George Benson, while his namesake, **John Marshall**, is the veteran English drummer who was born in 1941 in Isleworth, Middlesex.

A founding member of the jazz-rock band Nucleus, he has also played for other musicians and jazz and rock bands that include Soft Machine, Alexis Korner and Arthur Brown.

No live musical performance would be complete without proper amplification, and it is in this field that Marshalls have also made a name for themselves.

This is through the **Marshall Amplification**

Company, founded in the early 1960s by Jim Marshall – who began by selling percussion equipment from a small shop in Hanwell, London, before branching out into the range of specialist amplifiers used today by some of the world's top musicians.

Bearers of the Marshall name have also excelled, and continue to excel, in the highly competitive world of sport.

On the fields of European football, **David Marshall** is the Scottish goalkeeper who was born in Glasgow in 1985; at the time of writing a member of Scotland's international squad and goalkeeper for Cardiff City, he played for Celtic between 2002 and 2007.

Born in Avonbridge, Stirlingshire, in 1908, Dr James Marshall was the legendary Scottish professional footballer better known to his legions of fans as **Jimmy Marshall**.

First playing for Glasgow Shettleston, he joined Rangers in 1925 and stayed with the club for nine years – a period during which he also applied himself to successfully obtaining a medical degree.

Capped three times for Scotland, the talented

inside forward, who died in 1977, also played from 1934 to 1935 with London club Arsenal.

In the wholly different but no less skilled and strenuous sport of badminton, **Ethel Marshall** is the former American female player who has the distinction of having taken the U.S. Women's Singles title on the seven occasions that she contested it, between 1947 and 1953.

Born in 1924, she also took the U.S. Women's Doubles title, along with Beatrice Massman, in 1952 and 1956, the same year in which she was inducted into the U.S. Badminton Hall of Fame.

In the swimming pool, **John Marshall** was the noted Australian freestyle swimmer who was killed in a road accident at the age of only 27.

Born in 1930, he won the silver medal in the 1500-metres and a bronze in the 400-metres freestyle at the 1948 Olympics in London.

From swimming to the world of female professional wrestling, **Kristal Marshall**, born in 1983 in Los Angeles, is the model and former wrestler on the World Wrestling Entertainment circuit who was famed for her 'signature' tactic known as the 'Standing Hair Pull', while **Erin Marshall** is the British professional wrestler born in Southampton in 1987.

Also known by her ring name of Erin Angel, at the time of writing she is ranked as one of Britain's top eight female wrestlers.

Inducted into the Hockey Hall of Fame in the same year of his death in 1965, **Jack Marshall** was the Canadian ice hockey defenceman born in 1877 in Saint-Vallier, Quebec.

His long and distinguished career included playing for the Winnipeg Victorias, Montreal Hockey Club and Toronto Blueshirts, while among his other notable feats is that he was the first player to win six Stanley Cups.

In the cerebral world of chess, **Frank Marshall**, born in New York in 1877 and who died in 1944, was U.S. Chess Champion from 1909 to 1936.

Bearers of the Marshall name have also stamped their mark on the pages of world literature.

Born in 1902 in Noorat, Victoria, **Alan Marshall** was the Australian writer whose best-selling trilogy of autobiographical works are the 1955 *I Can Jump Puddles*, the 1962 *This is the Grass* and, from 1963, *In Mine Own Heart*; he died in 1984.

Also from Australia, **William Marshall**, born in 1944, is the crime and mystery writer best known for his *Yellowthread Street* series of novels, while in the United States **James Marshall**, born in 1942 in Texas, was the children's author and illustrator known for his *Fox and Miss Nelson* series of books; he died in 1992.

From prose to verse, **Jack Marshall** is the award-winning American poet who was born in 1936 in Brooklyn, New York, and whose acclaimed works include the 1971 *Floats* and the 2005 *From Baghdad to Brooklyn*.

Back to Australia, and in the world of medicine, **Barry Marshall**, born in 1951 in Kalgoorlie, Western Australia, is the leading international clinical microbiologist who in 2005 shared a Nobel Prize for research into specific bacteria thought to cause stomach ulcers.

In the world of economics, **Alfred Marshall**, born in London in 1842 and who died in 1924, was the author of the pioneering *Principles of Economics*, while in the field of sociology, Thomas Humphrey Marshall, better known as **T.H. Marshall**, was the British sociologist credited with first having introduced the concept of social rights.

The sociologist, who was born in 1893 and died in 1981, was the author of the influential essay collection *Citizenship and Social Class*.

It is one of the many cruel ironies of fate that, although responsible for setting in motion the great mid-nineteenth century California Gold Rush, **James Wilson Marshall** ended his days in poverty.

Born in 1810 in the township of Hopewell, New Jersey, by 1848 he was part-owner of a sawmill at Coloma, about 40 miles from Sutter's Fort on California's America River.

It was while using the natural force of the river to help to excavate and enlarge the tailrace for his mill that he spotted the glint of a number of shiny flecks.

These proved to be gold of the quality of 23 carats, or 96% purity, and news of the discovery soon spread like wildfire not only throughout California, but also around the world.

But it was a discovery that brought no benefit to Marshall as his employees abandoned him to join the search for gold, and his sawmill failed.

Forced off his land by the hordes of prospectors who descended, he attempted to start up a vineyard business, but this also failed, as did a later attempt at gold prospecting.

The California State Legislature granted him a small pension in 1872 in recognition of his role in this important period in the state's history, but this eventually lapsed after six years; living alone in a small cabin, he died destitute in 1885.

Marshall was buried at Coloma on a hill overlooking the America River, while a statue was erected depicting him pointing to the spot where he first made the discovery that changed his life for the worse.